✵ SMITHSONIAN

HABITATS OF THE WORLD

A BREATHTAKING VISUAL JOURNEY
THROUGH EARTH'S INCREDIBLE ECOSYSTEMS

WRITTEN BY
JOHN WOODWARD

CONSULTANT DR NICK CRUMPTON

DK

DK LONDON
Senior Editor Michelle Crane
Project Art Editor Kit Lane
Senior US Editor Kayla Dugger
Editorial Assistant Binta Jallow
Design Assistant Katy Jakeway
Production Editor Jacqueline Street-Elkayam
Senior Production Controller Poppy David
Jacket Designer Stephanie Cheng Hui Tan
Jacket Design Development Manager Sophia MTT
Managing Editor Francesca Baines
Managing Art Editor Philip Letsu
Publisher Andrew Macintyre
Associate Publishing Director Liz Wheeler
Art Director Karen Self
Publishing Director Jonathan Metcalf

Illustrators Andrew Beckett (Illustration X), Peter Bull, Barry Croucher (The Art Agency), Chris@KJA, SJC Illustration, Sofian Moumene

First American Edition, 2023
Published in the United States by DK Publishing
1745 Broadway, 20th Floor, New York, NY 10019

Copyright © 2023 Dorling Kindersley Limited
DK, a Division of Penguin Random House LLC
23 24 25 26 27 10 9 8 7 6 5 4 3 2 1
001–331820–Mar/2023

A catalog record for this book is available from
the Library of Congress.
ISBN 978-0-7440-6972-3

DK books are available at special discounts when purchased in bulk for sales promotions, premiums, fund-raising, or educational use. For details, contact: DK Publishing Special Markets, 1745 Broadway, 20th Floor, New York, NY 10019 SpecialSales@dk.com

Printed and bound in China

For the curious
www.dk.com

Smithsonian

Established in 1846, the Smithsonian is the world's largest museum and research complex, dedicated to public education, national service, and scholarship in the arts, sciences, and history. It includes 19 museums and galleries and the National Zoological Park. The total number of artifacts, works of art, and specimens in the Smithsonian's collection is estimated at 155.5 million.

MIX
Paper | Supporting
responsible forestry
FSC™ C018179

This book was made with Forest Stewardship Council™ certified paper—one small step in DK's commitment to a sustainable future.
For more information go to
www.dk.com/our-green-pledge

CONTENTS

World biomes

Wildlife habitats that extend over large areas are known as biomes. On land, each biome is defined by geography, climate, and vegetation. This map shows the distribution of the main biomes and picks out an example of each one.

Ice
Arctic and Antarctic seas freeze over in winter. But beneath the floating ice, the plankton-rich water teems with life.

Boreal forest
A band of evergreen, mainly coniferous forest extends all around the Arctic in the far north.

Desert
All but the driest, most hostile deserts support plants and animals adapted to cope with drought.

Mountain
High mountains such as the Andes have barren peaks but richer habitats on the lower slopes.

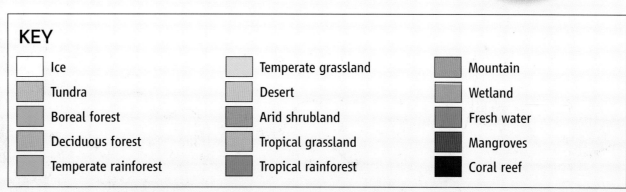

KEY

- ☐ Ice
- Tundra
- Boreal forest
- Deciduous forest
- Temperate rainforest
- Temperate grassland
- Desert
- Arid shrubland
- Tropical grassland
- Tropical rainforest
- Mountain
- Wetland
- Fresh water
- Mangroves
- Coral reef

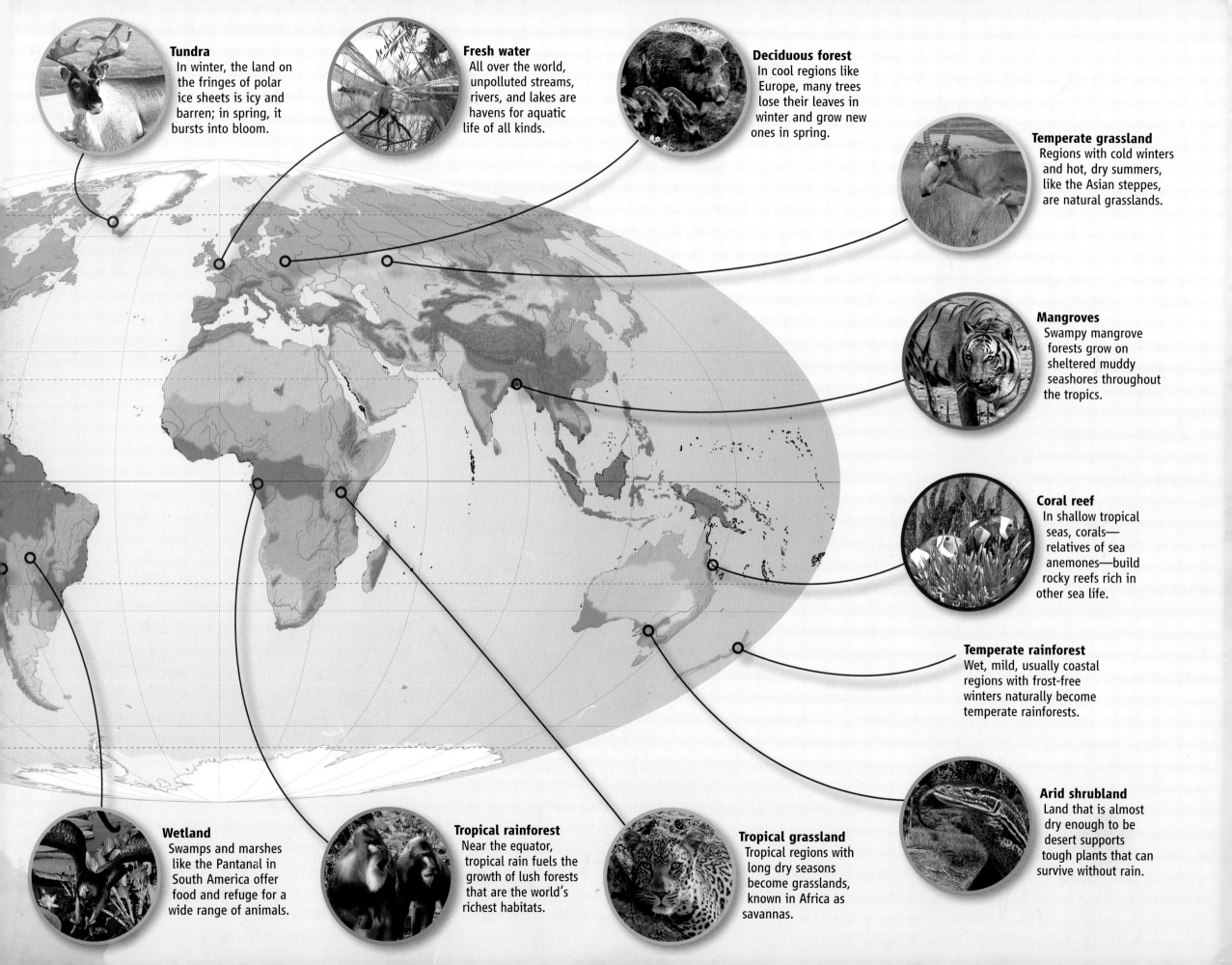

Tundra
In winter, the land on the fringes of polar ice sheets is icy and barren; in spring, it bursts into bloom.

Fresh water
All over the world, unpolluted streams, rivers, and lakes are havens for aquatic life of all kinds.

Deciduous forest
In cool regions like Europe, many trees lose their leaves in winter and grow new ones in spring.

Temperate grassland
Regions with cold winters and hot, dry summers, like the Asian steppes, are natural grasslands.

Mangroves
Swampy mangrove forests grow on sheltered muddy seashores throughout the tropics.

Coral reef
In shallow tropical seas, corals—relatives of sea anemones—build rocky reefs rich in other sea life.

Temperate rainforest
Wet, mild, usually coastal regions with frost-free winters naturally become temperate rainforests.

Arid shrubland
Land that is almost dry enough to be desert supports tough plants that can survive without rain.

Wetland
Swamps and marshes like the Pantanal in South America offer food and refuge for a wide range of animals.

Tropical rainforest
Near the equator, tropical rain fuels the growth of lush forests that are the world's richest habitats.

Tropical grassland
Tropical regions with long dry seasons become grasslands, known in Africa as savannas.

The *steephead parrotfish* crunches coral with its tough beaklike jaws to get at the soft parts and tiny seaweeds that grow in the crevices.

The parrotfish is attended by small *bluestreak cleaner wrasses* that do it a favor by picking parasites and dead skin off its body and gills.

The *clownfish* is immune to the stinging cells in a sea anemone's tentacles, so it can hide among them to stay safe from bigger fish that might eat it.

Bigeye trevally

Box jellyfish

Coral trout

Steephead parrotfish

Bluestreak cleaner wrasse

Clownfish

Sea anemone

Peacock mantis shrimp

Nudibranch

Giant triton

Crown-of-thorns starfish

Armed with a pair of clublike forelimbs, the *peacock mantis shrimp* smashes the shells of clams and crabs to get at the meat inside.

The prickly *crown-of-thorns starfish* eats coral, stripping parts of the reef bare. But it is eaten in turn by the giant triton sea snail.

A *turtle-headed sea snake* uses its ribbonlike tail to swim over the reef, searching for eggs that fish have laid among the coral.

Patrolling the deeper water between the corals, a *blacktip reef shark* snaps up reef fish, cuttlefish, and any other animals it can catch.

CORAL REEF
Great Barrier Reef, Australia

Extending for 1,430 miles (2,300 km) along the northeast coast of Australia, the Great Barrier Reef is the world's biggest coral reef. It has been built up over thousands of years by millions of living corals—relatives of sea anemones that support their bodies with stony skeletons. The sunlit reef provides a habitat for a dazzling diversity of colorful reef fish and other animals.

Turtle-headed sea snake

Exquisite wrasse

Broadclub cuttlefish

Blacktip reef shark

Biscuit sea star

Clown triggerfish

Green sea turtle

Emperor angelfish

Butterfly fish

Giant clam

Blue-ringed octopus

Brain coral

A *brain coral* is made up of many animals living in a colony. Microscopic algae in their tissues use the Sun's energy to make food that feeds the coral.

Growing in a crevice in the reef, a *giant clam* can live for a century or more and reach a colossal 47 in (120 cm) long.

Named for the electric-blue rings on its skin, the *blue-ringed octopus* has a venomous bite that can kill a human within a few minutes.

The muddy creeks threading through the mangroves provide perfect hunting territory for the massively powerful *saltwater crocodile*.

The *Asian openbill stork* preys mainly on snails that it gathers from shallow water with its long bill.

Mangrove branches make ideal daytime roosts for the big fruit-eating bats known as *flying foxes*.

A *Bengal tiger* stalks a big male chital, or spotted deer. The Sundarbans form one of the tiger's last surviving strongholds.

Common kingfisher

Flying fox

Brahminy kite

Asian openbill stork

Bengal tiger

Black-headed ibis

Little egret

Saltwater crocodile

Masked finfoot

Mangrove horseshoe crab

Fishing cat

Chital

Fiddler crab

Mudskipper

Mangrove mud crab

Northern river terrapin

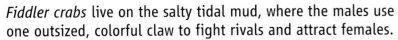

Fiddler crabs live on the salty tidal mud, where the males use one outsized, colorful claw to fight rivals and attract females.

Mudskippers are fish that spend most of their time out of water, on the mud. They carry a supply of water with them so they can breathe.

An *Indian python*—one of the world's biggest snakes—retreats to a tree as the incoming tide floods the muddy shoreline.

Rhesus macaques live in the treetops, feeding on fruit, nuts, and buds. If necessary, they can swim from one tree to another.

MANGROVES
Sundarbans, Bay of Bengal

Throughout the tropics, sheltered tidal shores support forests of salt-tolerant mangrove trees. They can grow in the waterlogged mud thanks to specially adapted roots that gather air at low tide. The world's biggest mangrove forest is the Sundarbans, which extends across the Ganges Delta in the Bay of Bengal. It is a refuge for a rich variety of animal life, including the endangered Bengal tiger.

Rhesus macaque

Indian python

Brown-winged kingfisher

Asian water monitor

Cotton pygmy goose

Ganges river dolphin

White-bellied sea eagle

Archerfish

Mangrove whipray

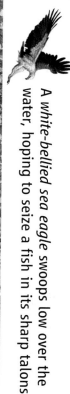

The *Ganges river dolphin* uses echolocation to find fish and other prey in the muddy water.

A *white-bellied sea eagle* swoops low over the water, hoping to seize a fish in its sharp talons.

The *fishing cat* lives up to its name by preying on fish. It may even dive into the water to chase after them like an otter.

The extraordinary *archerfish* shoots jets of water at insects perched on the exposed mangrove roots, knocking them into the water below.

1 Family groups of *African forest elephants* roam beneath the trees, gathering leaves, fruit, and tree bark. But adult males often live alone.

2 Strong enough to rip a monkey from its perch high in a tree, the *crowned eagle* is one of the forest's most fearsome predators.

TROPICAL RAINFOREST
Gabon, Central Africa

Lying on or near the equator, tropical rainforests are always warm and wet, with no cold or seriously dry seasons. This enables plants to keep growing fast all year round, creating the richest land habitats on Earth. The many layers of the forest support a huge variety of animals. In western Central Africa, they include forest elephants, leopards, gorillas, agile monkeys, and a colorful chorus of birds.

12 Gabon is the stronghold of the *mandrill*, a big monkey with a vividly colored face—especially the male.

11 Discovered as recently as 1988, the *sun-tailed guenon* lives only in the remote forests of central Gabon.

Kapok

Rosy bee-eater

Straw-colored fruit bat

African teak

Black-and-white-casqued hornbill

Red-bellied paradise flycatcher

Chocolate-backed kingfisher

Forest buffalo

Gray-necked rockfowl

Yellow-backed duiker

African golden cat

Tarantula

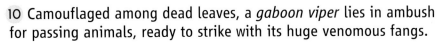

10 Camouflaged among dead leaves, a *gaboon viper* lies in ambush for passing animals, ready to strike with its huge venomous fangs.

9 A *red river hog* uses its strong, mobile snout to plow up the ground in search of juicy roots and burrowing animals.

 3 The *mantled guereza*—a leaf-eating colobus monkey—spends most of its life up in the tree canopy, high above the forest floor.

 4 Found throughout Central Africa, the *grey parrot* favors dense forests, where it searches the trees for fruit, nuts, and small animals.

5 A *white-bellied tree pangolin* uses its long tongue to lap up ants and termites foraging in the treetops.

6 Magnificent *western lowland gorillas* spend a lot of their time on the ground, eating leaves and fruit.

Great blue turaco

De Brazza's monkey

White-collared mangabey

Chimpanzee

Tree fern

Moustached guenon

 8 A prowling *leopard* might seem like a threat to the bongo, but it usually targets much smaller prey that is easier to kill.

 7 A large forest antelope, the *bongo* seeks out disturbed areas of forest where it can feast on the new growth of leaves and green shoots.

A big *baobab* tree can gather up to 32,000 gallons (120,000 liters) of water during the rainy season and store it in its massive trunk.

 Reaching 56 mph (90 kph) or more in a few seconds, a *cheetah* streaks across the grass in pursuit of a gazelle.

TROPICAL GRASSLAND
Serengeti, East Africa

Vast areas of the tropics have long dry seasons that prevent the growth of forests. They have become seas of grass dotted with specialized trees that are adapted to survive drought. In Africa, these grasslands support vast herds of grazing antelopes and zebras, which are hunted by powerful predators including cheetahs, lions, leopards, and spotted hyenas.

A pride of *lions* relax on an outcrop, the females having hunted successfully hours earlier.

A *lilac-breasted roller* watches the ground from a perch, ready to seize an insect or small lizard.

Baobab tree

Black rhino

White-backed vulture

Lilac-breasted roller

Spotted hyena

Lion

Aardvark

Termite mound

Cheetah

Warthog

Rock hyrax

Hippopotamus

Olive baboon

Dung beetle

African rock python

 Heaps of dung left behind by the grazing herds are gathered by busy *dung beetles*, which roll it away and bury it to feed their young.

 Growing to 20 ft (6 m) or more, an *African rock python* can squeeze an antelope to death and then swallow it whole—horns and all.

At up to 20 ft (6 m), a male *Masai giraffe* is the tallest living animal. It can gather leaves from the very tops of acacia trees.

In the dry season, when food is harder to find, the massively strong *African bush elephant* uproots trees to get at their leaves.

Verreaux's eagle

Lesser masked weaver bird

Leopard

Masai giraffe

Acacia tree

African bush elephant

Plains zebra

Nile crocodile

Wildebeest

Secretarybird

Thomson's gazelle

Black mamba

Grass rat

Wildebeest—a type of antelope—graze on short grass exposed by zebras, which eat the longer grass.

Small *Thomson's gazelles* nibble the even shorter grass revealed by the grazing herds of wildebeest.

 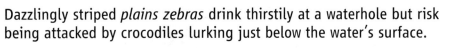 Dazzlingly striped *plains zebras* drink thirstily at a waterhole but risk being attacked by crocodiles lurking just below the water's surface.

 The long-legged *secretarybird* hunts on the ground, searching for insects, mice, and even venomous snakes.

1 The *snail kite* preys almost exclusively on the apple snails that live in the water, prying them from their shells with its long-hooked bill.

2 Trees growing between the pools attract dazzling birds like the *hyacinth macaw*—one of the world's largest parrots.

WETLAND
Pantanal, South America

Wetlands occur worldwide, wherever natural drainage is poor or rivers spill over into the surrounding landscape. The Pantanal is the world's largest tropical wetland, its pools and marshes covering 58,000 sq miles (150,000 sq km). It is a region of lush vegetation and teeming insect life that attracts a spectacular variety of animals.

Toco toucan

Giant waterlily

American purple gallinule

12 The Pantanal is a stronghold of the powerful *jaguar*, which dives into the water to seize prey.

11 The *green ibis* is one of many water birds that thrive in wetlands, including herons, storks, and kingfishers.

10 Family groups of *giant river otters* hunt fish below the floating leaves of giant waterlily. These sleek otters can grow to 6 ft (1.8 m) long.

9 Wading slowly forward, *roseate spoonbills* swing their specially adapted bills from side to side to sift tiny animals from the water.

3 The loud calls of *black howler monkeys* ring out across the wetlands. Only adult males are black, but both sexes howl.

4 Groups of *capybaras* wade in the shallows, gathering water plants. The semiaquatic, pig-sized capybara is the world's largest rodent.

Blue-and-yellow macaw

5 A skilled climber, an *ocelot* slips through tree branches in search of small animal prey.

6 Up to 10 million predatory *yacare caiman*, a type of alligator, live in the Pantanal.

Coati

Parrot snake

Marsh deer

South American tapir

Crab-eating fox

Boa constrictor

Water hyacinth

Green iguana

Paraguayan swimming frog

8 The astonishingly long toes of the *wattled jacana* spread its weight and allow it to walk on floating leaves of water plants without sinking.

7 *Ospreys* spend the northern winter hunting in the Pantanal. They prey on fish, plunging into the water to seize them.

A *red-tailed hawk* watches for prey before swooping down and attacking with its powerful claws.

The *cougar* is a stealthy hunter, hiding among the rocks and bushes and then ambushing its prey.

DESERT
Sonoran Desert, North America

Deserts are places that receive very little rainfall, but the Sonoran Desert gets more rain than most. For much of the time, only cacti, thorny shrubs, and small trees dot the dry sandy soil. But every so often, a rainstorm brings to life seeds that have been lying dormant for years. Suddenly, the desert bursts into bloom as short-lived plants all grow and flower at once. In the cool of the early morning, the desert is alive with animal activity.

The *velvet mesquite* is a thorny shrub that has deep roots to reach water stored underground.

Digging in the soil to find burrowing prey, this *American badger* will soon return to its den to sleep through the day.

Red-tailed hawk

Lesser goldfinch

Velvet mesquite

Ocotillo

Cougar

Roadrunner

Desert needlegrass

Pincushion cactus

White-throated woodrat

American badger

Ground squirrel

Ground squirrels dig burrows in the desert's sandy soil, where they hide from the heat of the day, emerging when it is cool to forage for food.

The speedy *roadrunner* is a bird that rarely flies. It races across the ground looking for small animals to eat.

Related to raccoons, *ringtails* are expert climbers. They are active at night and sleep in their dens in tree hollows during the day.

Costa's hummingbird sips nectar from a cactus flower. The strong-smelling flowers open in the night and only last for a single day.

Organ pipe cactus

Ringtail

Costa's hummingbird

Saguaro cactus

Gila woodpecker

Bighorn sheep

Staghorn cholla

Prickly pear

Plains bristlegrass

Western diamondback rattlesnake

Californian poppy

Horned lizard

Bark scorpion

Desert tortoise

The stem of a *saguaro cactus* swells to hold water soaked up by its shallow roots after rare rain showers.

A *horned lizard* basks in the morning sunlight. When it has warmed up, it will look for insects to eat.

 Ready to strike, the *western diamondback rattlesnake* bares its venomous fangs. After killing its prey, the snake swallows it whole.

 The *desert tortoise* uses its large shovel-shaped front feet to dig burrows in the soil, where it can shelter from the extreme heat.

 Propelled by its powerful feet, the *little grebe* dives beneath the surface to chase small animals that it can seize and swallow whole.

 A *gray heron* stalks slowly through the shallow water near the riverbank, looking for a fish to spear with its long, sharp bill.

FRESH WATER
Upper Thames, Great Britain

Rivers and lakes occur worldwide in almost every type of landscape. They are magnets for wildlife, offering ideal conditions for water plants and small aquatic animals. These provide food for many fish, as well as water birds like the swans attracted to this European river. In spring, the air above the water glitters with mayflies, dragonflies, and damselflies that have spent most of their lives underwater as aquatic larvae.

Hatching *mayflies* dance in the air above the water for a few brief hours before mating and dying.

Uniquely, the *water spider* lives underwater in an air bubble trapped within its submerged web.

Mayfly

Sedge Warbler

Bearded reedling

Mute swan

Gray heron

Perch

Chub

Little grebe

Water milfoil

Grass snake

Northern pike

Water spider

Eurasian otter

Great diving beetle

Ramshorn snail

 Lurking in ambush among the submerged waterweed, a *northern pike* waits for a fish to swim within range of its sharp teeth.

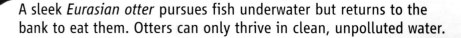 A sleek *Eurasian otter* pursues fish underwater but returns to the bank to eat them. Otters can only thrive in clean, unpolluted water.

An excellent swimmer, the *grass snake* often takes to the water in search of a meal—especially frogs, its favorite prey.

Male *emperor dragonflies* patrol the river, sparring with rivals and looking for females. They prey on other insects caught in flight.

Marsh harrier

Banded demoiselle

Emperor dragonfly

White willow

Swallow

Common moorhen

Mallard

Common frog

Eurasian coot

Water Vole

Common kingfisher

Bream

Roach

Three-spined stickleback

European eel

Swan mussel

Water voles nibble at juicy riverside plants and excavate their burrows in the riverbank.

A dazzling common kingfisher dives into the water from an overhanging perch to seize a fish.

The male *three-spined stickleback* builds a breeding nest on the riverbed and entices several females to lay their eggs in it.

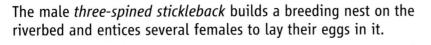
The snakelike *European eel* lives for many years in rivers, ponds, and lakes before migrating to the Atlantic Ocean to breed.

1 Winglike stretched skin between the legs of the *feathertail glider* allows it to glide from tree to tree in search of nectar and insects.

2 One of the few birds that hunts at night, the *spotted nightjar* pursues moths and other flying insects, seizing them on the wing.

12 Groups of *western gray kangaroos* feed mainly at night, eating a variety of grasses and leaves.

11 The *western pygmy possum* feeds almost exclusively on sugary, fragrant flower nectar and pollen.

Boobook owl

Silky mouse

Mitchell's hopping mouse

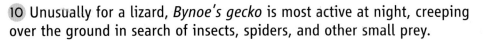

10 Unusually for a lizard, *Bynoe's gecko* is most active at night, creeping over the ground in search of insects, spiders, and other small prey.

9 The spiny, ant-eating *short-beaked echidna* is one of the few mammals that reproduces by laying eggs. If threatened, it curls into a prickly ball.

3 The flightless *emu* eats grasses, seeds, and insects. It usually forages in pairs, sometimes walking long distances to find food.

4 *Splendid fairywrens* nest in low, thorny shrubland. The young from previous broods help the female and bright blue breeding male collect food.

ARID SHRUBLAND
Victorian mallee, Australia

Regions with rare rainfall and hot summers are often colonized by woody plants with tough, leathery, drought-resistant leaves. They include the sagebrush of Californian chaparral, the aromatic herbs of Mediterranean garrigue, and the eucalyptus shrubs and small trees of Australian mallee. In the mallee, many mammals feed only at night, while most birds and reptiles are active by day.

Major Mitchell's cockatoo

Eucalyptus

White-winged chough

Red-capped robin

Emu-wren

Apostlebird

Galah

Australian painted lady

Eastern brown snake

Painted dragon

5 By day, the *purple-gaped honeyeater* gathers nectar from the flowers of bottlebrush and other shrubs.

6 The *sand goanna* is a big, powerful lizard that will prey on any animal smaller than itself.

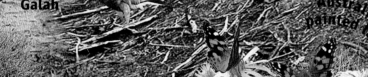

8 *Malleefowl* incubate their eggs in a heap of warm, rotting plants covered with sand, adding or removing sand to adjust the temperature.

7 If it senses danger, the *eastern blue-tongued skink* tries to scare its enemies away by hissing and flicking out its bright blue tongue.

A small herd of *taruca*, or north Andean deer, nibble the leaves of the scrubby plants that grow on the steep rocky slopes.

 Wading in a shallow lake, *James's flamingos* use their specialized bills to filter tiny algae from the water. The algae turn their feathers pink.

The blood of the *Andean goose* can absorb far more oxygen than usual, helping it fly in the thin air.

The *Vicuña* is adapted for life on the highest slopes. It has the same thick coat as the domestic alpaca.

Andean goose

Cochabamba mountain finch

Vicuña

Taruca

James's flamingo

Culpeo

Viscacha

Giant coot

 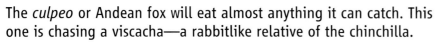 The *culpeo* or Andean fox will eat almost anything it can catch. This one is chasing a viscacha—a rabbitlike relative of the chinchilla.

 An *Andean hairy armadillo* digs in the dusty soil in search of seeds, juicy roots, insects, and other small burrowing animals.

The ostrichlike *lesser rhea* roams the grasslands in small groups, pecking at plants and small animals.

An *Andean condor*—the biggest of the vultures—soars on rising air currents with its huge wings outspread, looking for a meal.

A group of *guanacos* graze the damp ground near the lake. The guanaco is the wild ancestor of the domestic llama.

MOUNTAIN
Bolivian Andes, South America

The higher you climb above sea level, the colder it gets. This means that the tops of mountains like the Andes have almost polar climates, with barren, snowy peaks—even at the equator. Lower down, the landscape resembles Arctic tundra, with tough grasses and stunted trees growing among bare rock. The animals must contend with high winds, bone-chilling cold, and thin air, but they are well adapted to cope.

Andean condor

Queñoa tree

Lesser rhea

Guanaco

Diademed sandpiper-plover

Andean mountain cat

Chinchilla

Andean hairy armadillo

Andean flicker

Oddly for a woodpecker, the *Andean flicker* lives on high slopes with few trees and hunts on the ground.

 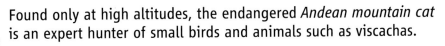 Found only at high altitudes, the endangered *Andean mountain cat* is an expert hunter of small birds and animals such as viscachas.

 Famous for its dense fur, the *chinchilla* is well insulated against the mountain chill. By day, it hides in a burrow or rock crevice.

Huge herds of the endangered *saiga antelope* once roamed the steppes. Their nostrils are specially adapted to filter dust from the dry air.

These grassy plains are the home of the heaviest flying bird, the *great bustard*. In spring, the males perform a spectacular courtship display.

TEMPERATE GRASSLAND
Kazakh steppe, Central Asia

Regions of the world that are not deserts yet are too dry to support forests develop into grasslands. Many occur in temperate zones that have warm summers but cold winters; they include the American prairies and pampas and the steppes of Europe and Asia. The animals that live on these grasslands are adapted to survive in open landscapes with nowhere to hide except underground and where water is often hard to find.

A *greater blind mole-rat* makes a brief visit to the surface before burrowing back into the dark.

The slender body of the *marbled polecat* enables it to hunt small animals in their burrows as well as out in the open.

Steppe falcon

Black-winged pratincole

Corsac fox

Saiga antelope

Great bustard

Greater blind mole-rat

Stone curlew

Eurasian hamster

Marbled polecat

Pallas's sandgrouse

Steppe tortoise

Steppe lemming

Common toad

Breeding male *Pallas's sandgrouse* visit pools to soak up water in their breast feathers and carry it back to their thirsty young.

The *steppe tortoise* spends the winter months asleep underground but emerges in spring to breed.

Elegant *demoiselle cranes* nest on the grasslands in summer, then migrate south over the Himalayas to escape the cold steppe winter.

Reintroduced to the steppes in the 1990s following near-extinction, *Przewalski's horse* now lives in wild herds like its ancestors.

Steppe eagle

Pallid harrier

Gray wolf

European bee-eater

Demoiselle crane

Przewalski's horse

Sociable plover

Feather grass

Orsini's viper

Viviparous lizard

Steppe marmot

The low-flying *pallid harrier* drifts slowly over the grasslands, searching for small animals.

Colorful *European bee-eaters* dart after their insect prey, seizing it in flight after a short chase.

A grassland specialist, *Orsini's viper* tracks small animals by scent and uses its venom to disable them before swallowing them whole.

Like most small mammals on the grasslands, the *steppe marmot* evades its enemies by taking refuge in a network of burrows.

1 Many of the oak trees are planted by the *European jay*, which gathers acorns (oak seeds) for winter food and buries them in the ground.

2 The Białowieża Forest is famous for its wild *European bison*, rescued from near-extinction and reintroduced to the forest in the 1950s.

Nuthatch

Oak tree

Hawfinch

White-

Common frog

Wood anemone

Orange-tip butterfly

12 *European robins* follow the wild boar to gather any worms and insect grubs they dig up.

11 *Wild boar* plow through the rich woodland soil in search of juicy nuts, fungi, and small animals.

10 Forced to spend the winter in hiding, the *European adder* emerges in spring to bask in the sunshine and find a breeding partner.

9 The *wood warbler* is one of many birds that arrive from Africa in spring to nest in the forest and feed their young on the teeming insect life.

3 *Tawny owls* roost in the trees by day and catch small animals at night. Hunting from perches, each owl sticks to its own territory.

 4 The short, rounded wings of the *sparrowhawk* enable it to dart between trees and branches to ambush and seize small birds.

DECIDUOUS FOREST
Białowieża Forest, Poland

In seasonal, temperate regions such as Northern Europe, many plants cope with winter frosts by lying dormant until spring. Soft-stemmed herbaceous plants die back to ground level, and deciduous trees such as oaks lose their leaves. When temperatures rise in spring, the plants burst into life, growing new, tender leaves that provide a feast for insects. These in turn attract migrant birds that fill the forest with birdsong.

5 A *Eurasian lynx* stalks a pair of unwary roe deer, which are among its favorite prey.

6 *Red deer* roam the forest, often grazing in open areas where they may be targeted by gray wolves.

Gray wolf

Roe deer

Bullfinch

Red squirrel

Lesser celandine

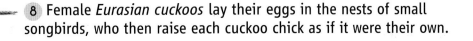 **8** Female *Eurasian cuckoos* lay their eggs in the nests of small songbirds, who then raise each cuckoo chick as if it were their own.

 **7** The agile *pine marten* pursues red squirrels through the trees, often leaping from branch to branch high above the ground.

The prickly *North American porcupine* feeds on leaves, berries, and bark in the treetops. Its spines help protect it from enemies.

A relative of martens and weasels, the tree-climbing *fisher* is one of the few hunters capable of killing a North American porcupine.

BOREAL FOREST
Central Canada

Also known as the taiga, the boreal forests of the far north extend all around the Arctic to the south of the tundra. They have long, cold, snowy winters and short summers, favoring evergreen conifer trees with frostproof, needlelike leaves. The climate means that the ground stays wet and boggy. In Canada, many of the resulting streams are turned into ponds by beavers.

The massively built *grizzly bear* feasts on berries and nuts in fall before sleeping through the winter.

Snow-white in winter, the *willow ptarmigan* has brown feathers for camouflage in summer.

North American porcupine

Fisher

American marten

Red squirrel

Grizzly bear

Black spruce

Caribou

Willow ptarmigan

Bald eagle

Beaver

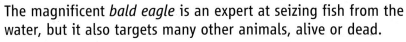
The magnificent *bald eagle* is an expert at seizing fish from the water, but it also targets many other animals, alive or dead.

Beavers fell trees with their big, chisel-like teeth and use them to dam streams, creating ponds that surround and protect their homes.

The *northern goshawk* is an ambush predator specialized for zipping between the trees to seize squirrels, chipmunks, and hares.

Incredibly sharp hearing enables the *great gray owl* to target mice and voles in near-darkness, even when they are hidden by deep snow.

Northern goshawk

Golden eagle

Great gray owl

Brown creeper

Red crossbill

White-winged crossbill

Black-backed woodpecker

Moose

American black bear

Red fox

Canada lynx

Snowshoe hare

Paper birch

Least chipmunk

Wolverine

The extraordinary twisted bill-tips of the *red crossbill* are a tool for prying the seeds out of pine cones.

American black bears are good climbers and often retreat to trees to avoid bigger, fiercer grizzly bears.

 In fall, rival male *moose* clash antlers as they compete over females. Known in Europe as elk, they are the biggest living deer.

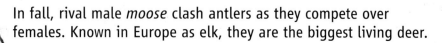

 Found all around the Arctic, the *wolverine* is a big, powerful weasel relative that hunts on the ground but also scavenges like a hyena.

Caribou—also known as reindeer—graze plants exposed by the melting snow. Most of the males have already shed their imposing antlers.

Specialized for life in the high Arctic, the *gyrfalcon* is a bigger relative of the peregrine that preys on birds and small mammals.

Lemmings are the staple prey of the *Arctic fox*, which loses its thick white winter coat in summer.

The *northern collared lemming* lives beneath the snow in winter, insulated from freezing Arctic winds.

TUNDRA
Western Greenland

The polar ice sheets are fringed by tundra—land that is frozen in winter but thaws out in spring. As the snow melts in Greenland, tough Arctic plants burst into bloom. The air starts to buzz with insect life, and animals that have survived the winter are joined by birds that fly north to nest and feed on the swarming insects.

Gyrfalcon

Caribou

Rock ptarmigan

Arctic fox

Purple saxifrage

Snow bunting

Northern collared lemming

Ringed plover

Ermine

Purple sandpiper

Groups of *Arctic hares* nibble tundra plants such as purple and yellow saxifrage while keeping a close eye on the wolves and foxes.

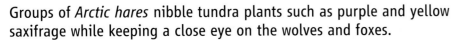

Still in its white winter camouflage, an *ermine* surprises a ringed plover. It will soon molt into its brown and white summer coat.

Packs of *Arctic wolves* prowl the tundra in search of prey. This pack is hoping to scatter a herd of musk oxen and seize one of their young.

 As the Arctic nights get shorter, the *snowy owl* hunts by day, mainly targeting small volelike lemmings that it can swallow whole.

Snowy owl

Musk oxen

Arctic wolf

Sanderling

Raven

Greenland white-fronted goose

Common loon

Red-necked phalarope

Heavyweight relatives of sheep and goats, hardy *musk oxen* live on the tundra throughout the year.

A hungry *raven* picks at the bones of an animal that has failed to survive the harsh Arctic winter.

 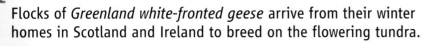 Flocks of *Greenland white-fronted geese* arrive from their winter homes in Scotland and Ireland to breed on the flowering tundra.

 The edge of a pool makes a perfect nest site for a *common loon*, which is so specialized for swimming that it can barely walk.

The mighty *bowhead whale* plows through plankton swarms with its huge mouth open, filtering the tiny creatures from the icy water.

Distinguished by its magnificent tusks, the *walrus* hunts in shallow coastal waters, diving to the sea bed to devour clams and other prey.

POLAR SEA
Beaufort Sea, Northern Canada

Frozen all winter, the Beaufort Sea might seem like a hostile habitat for life. But the water is rich in minerals vital to plant growth, and when the ice starts melting in spring, the sunlight fuels a bloom of plantlike plankton that feeds swarms of tiny animals. These are eaten by fish, which in turn feed seabirds, seals, whales, and polar bears.

The white skin of the *beluga whale* camouflages it among the sea ice, helping conceal it from prowling polar bears and hunting packs of killer whales.

Black-legged kittiwake

Common eider

Walrus

Beluga whale

Bowhead whale

Gray whale

Black guillemot

Long-tailed duck

Pacific herring

Spotted seal

Pacific sleeper shark

The *spotted seal* hunts fish such as Arctic cod and Pacific herring beneath the scattered ice floes drifting in open water.

Named for its slow-moving habits, the *Pacific sleeper shark* creeps up on fish, squid, and octopus and sucks them into its big mouth.

Like many Arctic birds, the *red-necked phalarope* is a summer breeding visitor. Unusually, the females are more colorful than the males.

Polar bears roam the sea ice in search of seal prey. The bears often ambush seals as they surface through holes in the ice to breathe.

Red phalarope

Red-necked phalarope

King eider

Red-throated loon

Polar bear

Ringed seal

Lion's mane jellyfish

Plankton

Pacific chum salmon

Arctic cod

Female *ringed seals* nurse their young in snow caves on the ice. But polar bears can detect them by smell and may punch their way in to grab a meal.

The *lion's mane jellyfish* drifts through the water, trailing long, venomous tentacles to snare fish, shrimp, and other prey.

Pacific chum salmon spend most of their lives feeding at sea, mainly on other fish. After five years, they swim upriver to spawn and then die.

PREDATORS AND PREY

In any habitat, plants or plantlike algae produce food that is eaten by animals. The animals use a lot of the energy in the food to fuel their activities, and only some of it is converted into body tissue that can be eaten by predators. This limits the number of predators and explains why top predators such as wolves are so much rarer than plant eaters, as this energy pyramid based on the Arctic tundra shows.

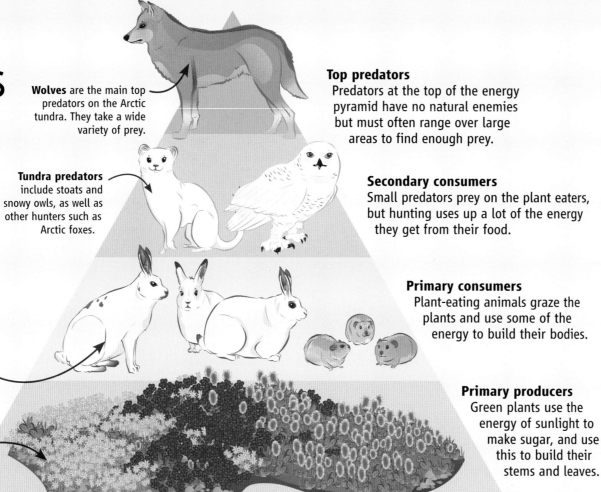

Wolves are the main top predators on the Arctic tundra. They take a wide variety of prey.

Top predators
Predators at the top of the energy pyramid have no natural enemies but must often range over large areas to find enough prey.

Tundra predators include stoats and snowy owls, as well as other hunters such as Arctic foxes.

Secondary consumers
Small predators prey on the plant eaters, but hunting uses up a lot of the energy they get from their food.

Arctic hares and volelike lemmings are the main small plant eaters on the Arctic tundra.

Primary consumers
Plant-eating animals graze the plants and use some of the energy to build their bodies.

Low-growing plants such as saxifrages grow and flower on the Arctic tundra during the summer.

Primary producers
Green plants use the energy of sunlight to make sugar, and use this to build their stems and leaves.

FOOD WEBS

Some plants and animals interact in a simple food chain. Seeds are eaten by mice, which are eaten in turn by owls. But the natural world is usually more complex than this, with each animal eating more than one type of food. This creates a food web, instead of a simple chain, as in this example from icy Arctic seas.

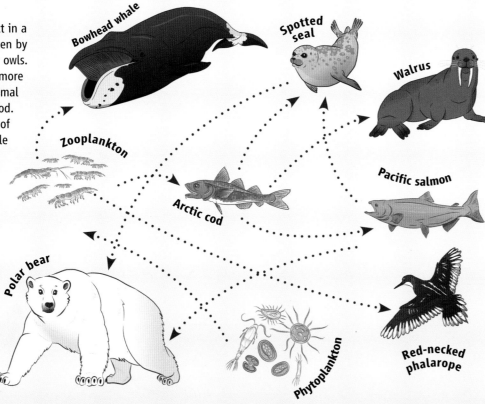

Zooplankton such as krill feed on microscopic algae that drift in the water as phytoplankton.

Arctic cod prey on the zooplankton, as well as eating small fish and other animals.

Polar bears hunt seals and their young, but also catch big fish, including Pacific salmon. Nothing preys on polar bears.

The bowhead whale is adapted to strain tiny shrimplike zooplankton from the water.

Spotted seals pursue and eat midsized fish such as Arctic cod, but also take crabs and shrimp.

The walrus feeds mainly on the clams and crabs that live on the sea floor, but also eats fish.

Pacific salmon hunting at sea prey on fish such as Arctic cod, as well as smaller fish.

Red-necked phalaropes are small ocean birds that prey on tiny zooplankton.

ACKNOWLEDGMENTS

Smithsonian Enterprises:
Product Development Manager Kealy Gordon
Director, Licensed Publishing Jill Corcoran
Vice President, Business Development & Licensing Brigid Ferraro
President Carol LeBlanc

Smithsonian reviewer:
Collections Manager, Division of Mammals, National Museum of Natural History Darrin Lunde

Dorling Kindersley would like to thank: **Additional editorial and design** Carron Brown, Sheila Collins, Simon Mumford, Jenny Sich; **Creative retouching** Steve Crozier and Stefan Podhorodecki; **Indexer** Elizabeth Wise; **Visualization** Rob Perry

The publisher would also like to thank the following for their kind permission to reproduce their images:
Andrew Beckett (Illustration X) pp.8–13; **Peter Bull** pp.14–15; **Chris@KJA Artists** pp.6–7, 18-25; **Barry Croucher (The Art Agency)** pp.26–27, 30–31; **Stuart Jackson Carter** pp.16–17; **Sofian Moumene** pp.4–5, 28–29

All other images © Dorling Kindersley
For further information see: www.dkimages.com